06- 311

S0-AXO-347

School
Library Media Center
...ton. CT. 00...

31

OCEAN

EDWARD R. RICCIUTI

BENCHMARK BOOKS

MARSHALL CAVENDISH
NEW YORK

Benchmark Books
Marshall Cavendish Corporation
99 White Plains Road
Tarrytown, New York 10591-9001

©Marshall Cavendish Corporation, 1996

Series created by Blackbirch Graphics, Inc.

All rights reserved. No part of this book may be reproduced or utilized in
any form or by any means electronic or mechanical including photocopy-
ing, recording, or by any information storage and retrieval system, without
permission from the copyright holders.

Printed and bound in Hong Kong.

Library of Congress Cataloging-in-Publication Data

Ricciuti, Edward R.
    Ocean / by Edward R. Ricciuti.
        p.   cm. — (Biomes of the world)
    Includes bibliographical references and index.
    ISBN 0-7614-0079-6 (lib. bdg.) ISBN 0-7614-0078-8 (set)
    1. Ocean—Juvenile literature. [1. Ocean.] I. Title. II. Series.
GC21.5.R516   1995
551.46—dc20
                                            95-4064
                                              CIP
                                              AC

Contents

Introduction

People traveling in an airplane often marvel at the patchwork patterns they see as they look down on the land. Fields, forests, grasslands, and deserts, each with its own identifiable color and texture, form a crazy quilt of varying designs. Ecologists—scientists who study the relationship between living things and their environment—have also observed the repeating patterns of life that appear across the surface of the earth. They have named these geographical areas biomes. A biome is defined by certain environmental conditions and by the plants and animals that have adapted to these conditions.

The map identifies the earth's biomes and shows their placement across the continents. Most of the biomes are on land. They include the tropical rainforest, temperate forest, grassland, tundra, taiga, chaparral, and desert. Each has a unique climate, including yearly patterns of temperature, rainfall, and sunlight, as well as certain kinds of soil. In addition to the land biomes, the oceans of the world make up a single biome, which is defined by its salt-water environment.

Looking at biomes helps us understand the interconnections between our planet and the living things that inhabit it. For example, the tilt of the earth on its axis and wind patterns both help to determine the climate of any particular biome.

The climate, in turn, has a great impact on the types of plants that can flourish, or even survive, in an area. That plant life influences the composition and stability of the soil. And the soil, in turn, influences which plants will thrive. These interconnections continue in every aspect of nature. While some animals eat plants, others use plants for shelter or concealment. And the types of plants that grow in a biome directly influence the species of animals that live there. Some of the animals help pollinate plants. Many of them enrich the soil with their waste.

Within each biome, the interplay of climatic conditions, plants, and animals defines a broad pattern of life. All of these interactions make the plants and animals of a biome interdependent and create a delicate natural balance. Recognizing these different relationships and how they shape the natural world enables us to appreciate the complexity of life on Earth and the beauty of the biomes of which we are a part.

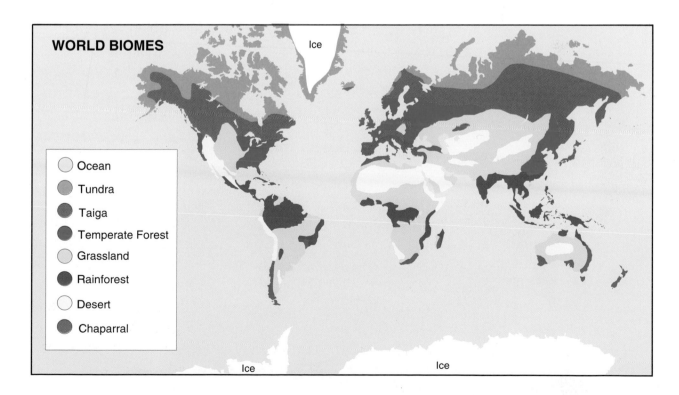

WORLD BIOMES

Ice

○ Ocean
● Tundra
● Taiga
● Temperate Forest
○ Grassland
● Rainforest
○ Desert
● Chaparral

Ice   Ice

1

The World Ocean

Imagine that the earth is a smooth ball, with no mountains or valleys. If so, the entire planet would be covered by seawater 12,000 feet deep (3,660 meters). Actually, the surface of the earth *is* mostly liquid. The ocean biome extends over more of the earth's surface than do all the other biomes combined. About 71 percent of the planet, in fact, is covered by ocean. Land biomes and fresh waters account only for the remaining 29 percent.

**Opposite:
The ocean covers more than 70 percent of the earth.**

The Largest Biome

The ocean dwarfs all the other biomes in the amount of area it has in which to support living organisms—a total of 329 million cubic miles (1,316 million cubic kilometers). The ocean biome is deeper than the tallest mountains on Earth are high.

If Mount Everest were placed into the ocean depths, its peak would be submerged under more than a mile of water.

Scientists are able to determine ocean depth by the amount of time it takes sound to reach the bottom. They have used oceanographic research vessels to beam sound waves to the ocean floor in order to find its depth in various locations. Sound travels at a speed of 1,129 feet (344 meters) per second in water. In 1876, when the British research vessel *Challenger* sent a sound signal to the bottom of the Pacific Ocean off the island of Guam, it took 7.25 seconds for the signal to reach its target. This told the scientists that the depth, now called the Challenger Deep, was 35,640 feet (10,870 meters). On July 23, 1960, the undersea research craft *Trieste* descended into the sea not far from the Challenger Deep and reached the bottom at 35,800 feet (10,919 meters).

Other very deep areas of the ocean have been found off the South Pacific island of Tonga (34,884 feet [10,639 meters]), in the Indian Ocean off Java (25,344 feet [7,730 meters]), and in the Atlantic Ocean off Puerto Rico (28,347 feet [8,646 meters]). Most of the ocean is darker than the blackest night, because as sunlight passes through water, it is absorbed very quickly. Even in the clearest water, light begins to dim at a depth of about 200 feet (61 meters). Below 300 feet (92 meters), there is not enough light for plants to grow. At a depth of close to 1,000 feet (305 meters), the last traces of light vanish. From the dark depths to the wave-tossed surface, virtually all areas of the ocean support some form of living things.

Landscape Under the Waves

The vast area of salt water that encircles all of the world's continents is often called the World Ocean. It, in turn, is divided into a number of major oceans: the Pacific, Atlantic, Indian, Arctic, and, according to some geographers, the Antarctic. (Other geographers view the Antarctic Ocean as an extension of the Pacific, Atlantic, and Indian oceans.) Each major ocean has extensions and arms known as seas, the boundaries of which are determined by islands, peninsulas, and other landforms. The East China Sea, for instance, is an extension of the Pacific, while the Sea of Japan is known as an arm. The Mediterranean Sea is thought of as an arm of the Atlantic, while the Caribbean Sea is one of the Atlantic's extensions.

Although the surface of the ocean does not change much in its appearance, the landscape of the ocean floor is as varied as the land. Much of the ocean bottom that is far from land has vast, flat plains cut by sheer, deep canyons called ocean trenches. The Challenger Deep, for example, lies in an undersea canyon known as the Marianas Trench. Rising from the ocean bottom are underwater peaks known as seamounts, some of which are higher than any mountains on land. When a seamount thrusts through the surface of the ocean, it becomes an island. The Hawaiian islands are examples of seamounts that have become islands. Running along the bottoms of most oceans are parallel ranges of underwater mountains called oceanic ridges, which are separated by immense valleys. Many of these ridges exist in a series that has a combined length of up to 40,000 miles (64,360 kilometers).

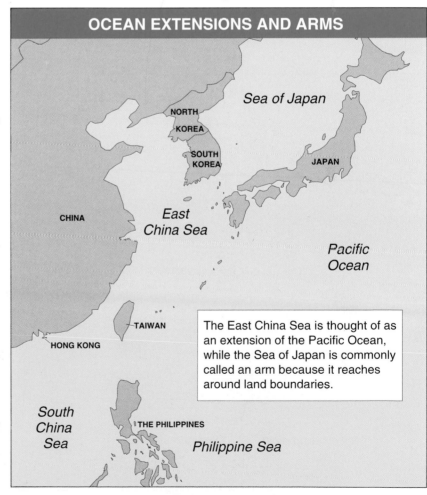

OCEAN EXTENSIONS AND ARMS

Sea of Japan

NORTH KOREA

SOUTH KOREA

JAPAN

CHINA

East China Sea

Pacific Ocean

TAIWAN

HONG KONG

South China Sea

THE PHILIPPINES

Philippine Sea

The East China Sea is thought of as an extension of the Pacific Ocean, while the Sea of Japan is commonly called an arm because it reaches around land boundaries.

Major Ocean Zones

Scientists divide the ocean into several zones, based on depth. At the land's edge, where the tide ebbs and flows, is the intertidal zone, which is shallow enough that at certain times during each day it is either below or above water. Where the intertidal zone ends, the continental shelf begins. It is a plain that slopes gently seaward from the lip of each continent and that totals 10 million square miles (25,900,000 square kilometers) in area. In some locations, such as off the coast of Newfoundland, the continental shelf extends as much as 300 miles (483 kilometers) from land. Over the course of thousands of years, the continental shelf has experienced the same rise and fall of the sea that the intertidal zone undergoes daily. During the Ice Age, sea level was much lower than it is today

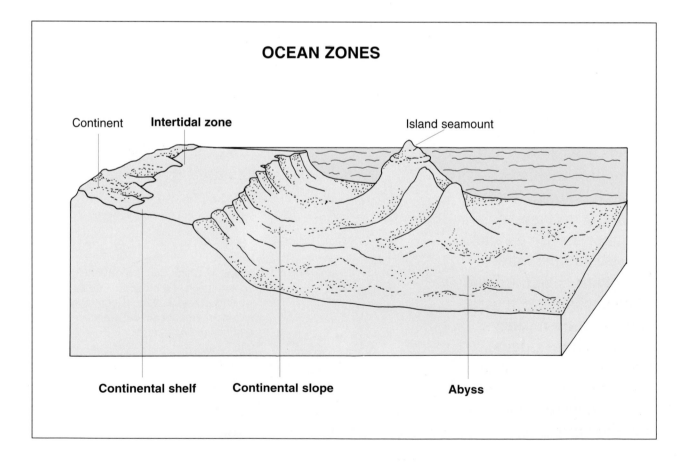

OCEAN ZONES

Continent   **Intertidal zone**   Island seamount

Continental shelf   **Continental slope**   **Abyss**

and large expanses of the continental shelf of North America were above water. Early peoples hunted mammoths in areas where fishing fleets hunt for codfish today. The waters above the continental shelf are the coastal waters of the continents.

At a depth of about 600 feet (183 meters), the gradual slant of the continental shelf becomes a sharp tilt toward the ocean floor. This is known as the continental slope. The slope plunges for about 12,000 feet (3,660 meters), where it meets the bottom of the ocean, or seabed, an area known as the abyss. Waters above the continental slope and the abyss form the open ocean, which, unlike the coastal waters, is not greatly affected by land.

Density and Life

If you have ever waded through water that is only 2 or 3 feet (0.6 to 0.9 meter) deep, you know that it takes more effort to move through water than it does to walk on land. That is because water molecules are packed together more tightly than air molecules—800 times more tightly, in fact. This means that water is 800 times thicker, or more dense, than air. This has a tremendous impact on all things that live in the ocean.

If you throw a stick of wood in the air, it will fall to the ground. But in the water, it will float. Because of its greater density, water provides more support for objects than air does. On land, a great blue whale would collapse under the weight of its 100-ton (91-metric-ton) body. Its bones and muscles would not be strong enough to hold up all that weight against the force of gravity. But in the ocean, the whale's immense body is supported by the water.

Many fish have an internal organ that allows them to adjust their buoyancy, or ability to float. This organ is called the swim bladder, a balloonlike bag that fish can either inflate or deflate. The more the swim bladder inflates, the higher the fish rises in the water; when it deflates, the fish can sink to a deeper level of the ocean. By keeping just the right amount of air in the swim bladder, a fish can even float in place.

The swim bladder also enables a fish to move around slowly for short distances without swimming and using up its energy. Some fish, such as sharks, lack a swim bladder and must constantly swim; otherwise they would sink to the bottom. Sharks, however, as well as many other creatures of the ocean biome, have a streamlined shape that makes it easier for them to push through water. This way they use less energy when they swim than they would if their bodies were not streamlined.

Sea Shapes

Suppose, for a moment, that you wanted to cut a stick of butter with a knife. Would you use the flat side of the knife? No. You would use the edge, which is thin and sharp. The bodies of most fish are built so that, when they swim, their leading edge presents a small amount of surface against the water. The flat bodies of the stingray and the butterfly fish are very narrow; top to bottom in the stingray's case, side to side in the case of the butterfly fish. Both slice through water like a knife through butter. The bodies of most sharks are shaped

Body shapes play an important role in the sea. Below left: The flat shape of a stingray helps it to glide through water. Below right: A moray eel's body is perfect for slipping in and out of rocks and coral.

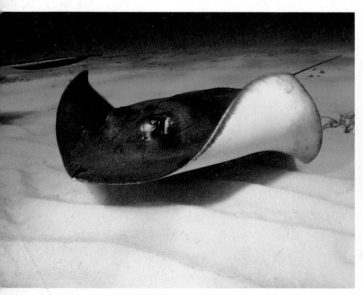

somewhat like torpedoes, tapering toward the snout. Even more torpedo-shaped are the bodies of tuna. This body shape enables a fish to push water aside and slip through it with ease. The moray eel's long, narrow body enables it to glide through water like a snake.

The body of a fish has many muscles arranged in a line from head to tail. If you have ever caught a fish and tried to take it off the hook, you know that its body, besides being slippery, is very powerful and flexible. Most fish propel themselves through the water by moving their tail fins from side to side. The fin moves each time a fish flexes and unflexes a series of strong muscles in sequence from head to tail. This flexing motion is too fast for the human eye to see. In the water, when the tail fin flicks to the side, it propels the fish forward. Some fish, such as the boxfish, have rigid bodies. They use fins behind the head to swim.

Sailfish are among the fastest inhabitants of the ocean and can travel up to 60 miles (96 kilometers) per hour.

Some types of fish can swim as fast as automobiles travel. Sailfish and swordfish have reached speeds of 60 miles (96 kilometers) an hour; marlin, bonito, and albacore can all swim 50 miles (80 kilometers) an hour; and the barracuda can attain speeds of 25 miles (40 kilometers) an hour. There are several other sea creatures that are rapid swimmers. Porpoises, for example, can swim at speeds of more than 20 miles (32 kilometers) an hour.

Porpoises and their relatives, the whales, also use their tails to swim. The tail, or flukes, of a whale moves up and down, not side to side like that of most fish. Sea lions swim with their front flippers, which are long and powerful. Seals use their rear flippers.

Breathing Under Water

Seawater, like all water, contains oxygen. Sea life—with a few exceptions—breathes the oxygen that is dissolved in water with organs called gills. Located slightly behind a fish's eyes, and on both sides of its body, gills contain tiny, thin-walled blood vessels. Oxygen in the seawater passes through the walls of these vessels into the fish's bloodstream. In return, carbon dioxide waste is carried from the bloodstream into the water in a similar manner.

Many ocean animals besides fish have gills. The gills of shrimp are feathery structures on the underside of the thorax, or chest. Sea mammals, such as whales and seals, cannot use dissolved oxygen; they must get it directly from the air. Whales breathe by surfacing and inhaling air through their nostrils, or blowholes, on top of their heads. When a large whale inhales, its huge lungs fill with an immense amount of air, often more than 100 cubic feet (2.8 cubic meters). This is enough to allow whales to hold their breath for almost an hour while underwater. Seals and sea lions also surface to breathe through their nostrils. Some of these mammals can hold their breaths for thirty minutes.

WHY THE SEA IS SALTY

Anyone who has opened his or her mouth while swimming in the ocean knows it is salty. There are several different salts in ocean water, but most of it—about 79 percent—is sodium chloride, common table salt. Scientists believe that salts have entered ocean water in two ways. First, when the ocean formed, salts probably dissolved from rock in the ocean floor. Then as time passed, more and more salts were washed into the sea from the land, a process that continues today. The saltiest parts of the ocean are in the tropics, far from land, where water evaporates quickly, building up salt concentrations. The least salty is in polar regions, where temperatures are frigid and melting ice dilutes the water.

The Ocean in Motion

Waves, tides, and currents keep ocean water constantly in motion. The wind causes the action of most waves. Currents, whether warm or cold, are ocean highways along which many types of creatures travel. The Gulf Stream is a current that is more than 50 miles (80 kilometers) wide, moves at up to 4 miles (6 kilometers) an hour, and circles the North Atlantic. In the summer, the Gulf Stream carries tropical water up past the coast of North America, bringing with it warm-water fish not found there in winter. Currents also churn the waters, mixing nutrients and making the sea richer in food.

Tides are created by the gravitational forces of the moon and the sun. The moon has the greater effect because of its nearness to the earth. The moon pulls at the waters of the ocean nearest to it, creating one bulge there and another on the opposite side of the earth. These bulges are the high tides, and halfway between them are the low tides. As the earth revolves around the sun, both high tides and low tides pass across the ocean—twice a day. The highest tidal ranges, called spring tides, occur twice a month when the sun and the moon are in a straight line with the earth. The lowest tidal ranges, called neap tides, occur when the sun and the moon are at right angles to the earth.

THE NOISY WORLD BENEATH THE WAVES

The underwater world of the ocean is sometimes referred to as the silent deep. This term, however, is not an accurate way to describe the ocean, because considerable noise exists beneath its surface. Many sea creatures produce sounds, and because sound travels so quickly in water, some of these sounds can be heard a long way off. Certain sounds made by whales travel for many miles.

Whales are among the noisiest creatures of the ocean. One species, the beluga whale, hoots, whistles, and squeals so much that it is sometimes called the sea canary. Sound is a means of communication for whales. Whales also use sound to navigate and find food. Many kinds of whales can emit rapid-fire clicks that are beamed at underwater objects, such as a rock pile or a school of fish. The whales can determine the location of such objects by the way sounds reflect from the objects and back to the whale. This is called echolocation.

A large number of fish produce sounds by grinding their teeth or vibrating the air in their swim bladders. Some fish even get their names from the sounds they make—drums and croakers, for example. Toadfish are known to whistle, and groupers make thumping noises. Scientists believe that at least some of the sounds made by fish are mating calls, and some may be used to frighten away enemies. Some ocean invertebrates—animals without backbones—can also be noisy creatures. Spiny lobsters chatter, and certain species of shrimp make snapping sounds.

Beluga whales use hoots, whistles, and squeals to communicate with members of their species.

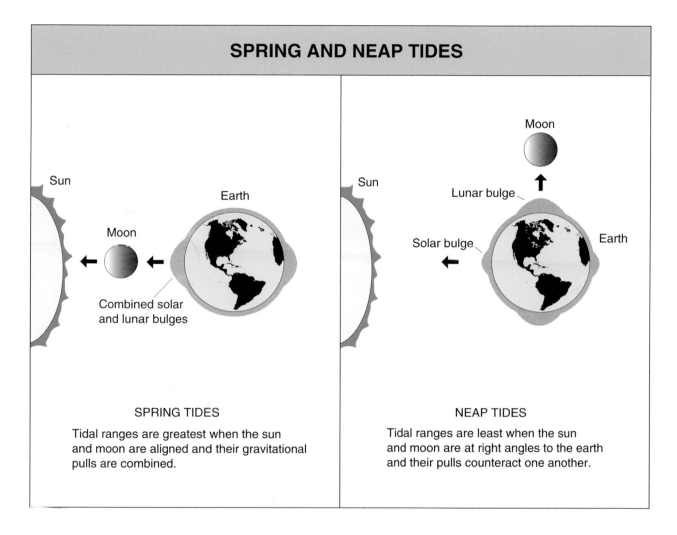

SPRING AND NEAP TIDES

SPRING TIDES

Tidal ranges are greatest when the sun and moon are aligned and their gravitational pulls are combined.

NEAP TIDES

Tidal ranges are least when the sun and moon are at right angles to the earth and their pulls counteract one another.

The area that the tides cover and uncover with water each day is the boundary of the ocean biome. It is also a battleground between the ocean and the land. Waves continually beat upon the land. The force of the water sweeps away soil and eats at rocks. The land, however, strikes back. Sand taken from one beach swirls through the water and reaches shore again, making a new beach. Rocks crumble into soil, creating new land. The cycle never ends. In the midst of this zone, a vast number of living things have made their home. Few other plants and animals in the natural world face a greater challenge to survival.

2

Life on the Shore

For the plants and animals that live in the intertidal zone of the ocean biome, life is not exactly a day at the beach. The shore is a harsh home for living things, a violent place hammered by surf, swept by winds, and with extreme ranges of temperature and moisture levels. Even so, the intertidal zone teems with life. One reason for this is that the intertidal zone is what scientists call an ecotone, a place where two very different environments meet—in this case, the land and the ocean.

A Changing World

Ecotones support a wide variety of living organisms because they offer a wide variety of habitats. This is especially true where land and sea meet. Such birds as puffins, which catch fish at sea and nest in burrows on cliffs, are very good

Opposite:
The shoreline
is a beautiful
area that pro-
vides a bounty
of habitats.

Puffins thrive
in the interface
between land
and sea, as they
find food in
the water and
shelter in shore-
line cliffs.

examples of creatures that use both the land and the ocean environments. So are sea lions, which come ashore to breed and have their young.

There are several types of shores: rocky, sandy, marshy, and swampy. Each one has its own population of plants and animals, all of which—especially those of the intertidal zone—share one trait in common: They have adapted to life in a place of continual change. Because of the regular advance and retreat of tides, organisms that inhabit the shore must be able to live both in and out of the water. For hours a day, intertidal zone organisms are protected at high tide by the water, which moderates temperature change. For hours at low tide, they may bake in the sun or be chilled by the cold. They must adapt, in order to survive.

Life on the Rocks

Intertidal organisms live in parallel belts, or zones, from low water to where the spray barely wets the land. These belts are usually named for the plant or animal most common there. The belts are most pronounced on rocky shores, such as those of New England and the Pacific Northwest. These belts look like stripes along cliff bases and boulders.

In New England, the uppermost belt is the black zone. The rocks are covered with a very slippery black scum that is really blue-green algae—simple, plantlike organisms that have edged out of the sea. The algae are moistened only by sea spray and storm waves, but that is enough to keep them wet. Below the black zone is the periwinkle zone, named for the rough periwinkles, or

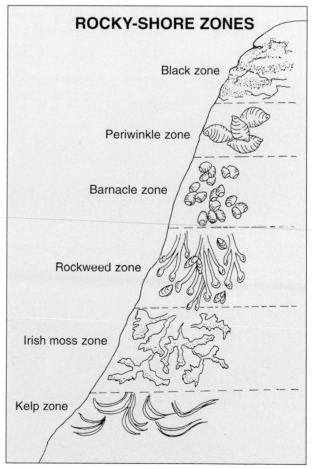

ROCKY-SHORE ZONES

Black zone

Periwinkle zone

Barnacle zone

Rockweed zone

Irish moss zone

Kelp zone

snails, that cover the rocks there. This zone is underwater only during the spring tides. When the snails are in danger of drying out, they seal themselves in their shells with a horny lid and conserve moisture. Most other sea snails can survive this way for only a few hours out of water, but the rough periwinkles can manage for several weeks.

Below the periwinkle zone is the barnacle zone, where the white conelike shells of these creatures carpet the rocks. Someone once likened a barnacle to a shrimp lying on its head in a box, and kicking food into its mouth with its feet. It is a good description. Barnacles do resemble shrimp and belong to the same group of animals, the crustaceans. The head of an adult barnacle is anchored in place on the rock with a powerful natural cement. The conelike shell that encloses it is made of material secreted by the barnacle. When the tide comes in, the barnacle opens a lid on top of the cone and sticks out its feathery feet. The feet sweep through the water and gather tiny plants and animals, on which the barnacle feeds. When the tide goes out, the barnacle—just like the periwinkle—closes its shell and keeps moisture inside.

Below the barnacle zone is another zone, one characterized by a seaweed called rockweed. This zone generally experiences high and low tides twice daily. Many barnacles and snails can be found there. The zone below the rockweed is marked by another seaweed called Irish moss. This zone is at the edge of the sea, and is exposed at low tide only for short periods. Mussels are often plentiful in this zone. Below the Irish moss zone is yet another, immediately below the low-water mark, called

Looking down on this cluster of barnacles, you can see the slits that open to allow their feet to emerge and gather food.

BEACHES COME AND GO

The sandy beach you see today is only temporary. Wind and water constantly shift and carry sand, destroying existing beaches and building new ones. This process has been closely studied on Assateague Island, off the coasts of Maryland and Virginia. The island started to form thousands of years ago, when waves picked up sand offshore and deposited it in shallows near the coast, creating a sandbar. The bar then trapped sand brought in by waves, while winds swirling over distant beaches blew in even more. Meanwhile, southerly currents lengthened the bar. Gradually, an island was formed, and beach grass took root, holding the sand in place. Today, Assateague Island continues to head southward as sand is taken from its northern beaches and deposited at its southern tip. On Cape Cod, in Massachusetts, a similar process is under way. The beaches on the northern tip of Cape Cod, in Provincetown, are gaining sand and building up. Those to the south, and on offshore islands, are losing sand.

Assateague Island is an example of a barrier island, which lies parallel to the coast and is backed by a bay. As Assateague grew, it protected the coast behind it from the power of the wind, surf, and storms. Between Assateague and the mainland, a bay formed. Shielded by the island from the full force of the ocean, the bay water's are quiet. Here, and on the bays of other barrier islands, sand and other sediments have collected, creating mud-bottomed shallows where plants that can tolerate salt grow.

the kelp zone. This zone really marks the beginning of the sea, and is inhabited by fish and other creatures that are not able to survive higher on the shore.

Being able to stay anchored in the pounding surf is a big advantage for an intertidal zone animal or plant. The relatives of jellyfish called sea anemones, whose colorful tentacles make them resemble flowers, each have a large "foot" that works like a suction cup and attaches to rock. Most of the plants in the rocky intertidal zone are seaweeds, which are a form of algae. They do not have roots, but with structures at the end of their stalks called holdfasts, many fasten to rocks and other objects. Large seaweeds called kelp have holdfasts resembling claws. Rockweeds have a padlike holdfast and air bladders on their fronds (shoots) to keep them afloat during the high tides.

Life in the Shifting Sands

Another type of seashore is the sandy beach, such as those beaches that dominate Cape Cod and the Atlantic coast from the southern shore of Long Island, New York, to Florida. Wind, waves, and tides swirl the surface sand, so that it is in constant motion. A sandy beach can look lifeless, except for gulls and such shorebirds as sandpipers. Under the sand, however, life abounds. Parchment worms filter food from the water and move through U-shaped burrows with their paddlelike appendages. Razor clams, sandworms, and tiny coquina clams also flourish on seashores in various regions.

Because so many creatures are hidden below the surface of the sand, life zones are not as easy to see on the sandy beach as they are on the rocks. Nonetheless, they do exist.

American dune grass dots the dune zone along a stretch of sandy beach in Cape Cod, Massachusetts.

The dune zone corresponds to the black zone of rocky shores. Plants, such as American dune grass, sea oats, and prickly pear cactus, root in the sand, which piles up around them, forming dunes. The plants hold the dunes together, but if the vegetation is destroyed, storm waves and winds can sweep the dunes away. Creatures of the dunes are mostly land animals, from tiger beetles to raccoons.

The ghost crab is an inhabitant of the upper beach zone.

Sea animals, such as the burrowing crustaceans called beach hoppers, begin to appear on the upper beach zone and are submerged only during storms and very high tides. The upper beach is the home of the ghost crab, which burrows as much as 4 feet (1.2 meters) into the sand. It breathes with gills, which it must keep wet. It does so by scurrying down to the edge of the waves, dashing in, and rocketing back to its burrow.

The middle beach zone is always subject to the tides, so sea creatures there must be able to withstand exposure to air for much of the day. Most—such as the mole crab, razor clam, and venus clam—survive by burrowing below the surface.

The lower beach zone is always covered by water, although it may be only a few inches deep at low tide. There, creatures that rarely emerge from the water, such as lady crabs, mix with those—flounder, for instance—that never do.

March Toward the Sea

When mudflats build up in protected shallows, certain plants that can withstand salt advance from the land toward the sea and anchor the mud in place, in much the same way that

25

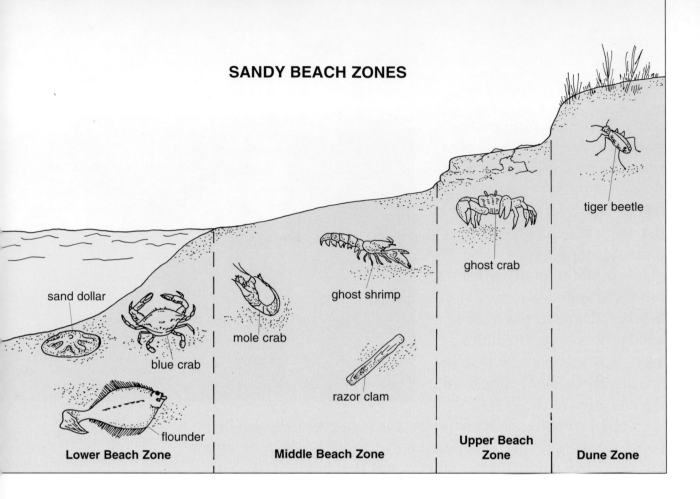

SANDY BEACH ZONES

sand dollar

blue crab

flounder

Lower Beach Zone

mole crab

ghost shrimp

razor clam

Middle Beach Zone

ghost crab

Upper Beach Zone

tiger beetle

Dune Zone

beach grass anchors the sand dunes. In temperate regions, salt marshes of such plants as cordgrass, sedge, and rush form. Along much of the North American coast, salt marsh cordgrass thrives, even though it is flooded twice daily with salt water. Salt marsh cordgrass is able to turn salt water, which enters through its roots, into fresh water. Salt is removed from the seawater by glands in the plant and is excreted through its leaves. Salt marsh cordgrass forms the main part of the marsh and is the plant that leads the march of land vegetation over mudflats toward the sea. A related, but not as salt-tolerant, cordgrass grows on higher ground, which is flooded only occasionally, during severe storms.

In southern Florida, and throughout the tropics, salt marshes are largely replaced by swamps of trees called mangroves. There are three main species of mangroves—white, black, and red. Although they are not related, all are able to grow close to, and even in, salt water. Like the other seashores, the mangrove swamp can be divided into zones. The mangrove that leads the march toward the sea is the red mangrove. It can survive in watery mud and tolerate being flooded by the tides because of its prop roots. These roots arch out from the branches, often 20 feet (6 meters) above the surface of the water. Black mangroves grow on slightly more solid mud, which is farther up the shore than the red. Like salt marsh cordgrass, black mangroves excrete salt through their leaves. The white mangrove is found on higher ground, flooded only during severe storms. These trees sometimes extend far inland.

Salt marshes and mangrove swamps are rich in nutrients that have been carried from the ocean by the tide and from the land by rivers and streams, at whose mouths, or estuaries, these wetlands also exist. Decomposed vegetation adds to the rich nutrient soup of these wetlands, which are very productive for living things. Small fiddler crabs feed on decaying marsh vegetation, while blue crabs charge out of the water to catch them. Some of the fish of the marshes and mangroves—such as a type of killifish called a mummichog—can live in water that is almost fresh, so they travel far, up rivers and creeks. Mussels, barnacles, and oysters cling to the roots of mangroves and are then eaten by starfish and a huge type of snail called a conch.

One of the world's most unusual fish lives in the mangroves of Africa, Asia, and Australia. The mudskipper uses its chest fins to hop about on the mudflats and even to crawl up

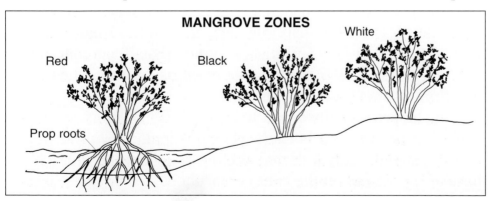

MANGROVE ZONES

White

Red

Black

Prop roots

Red mangroves have prop roots that protect them from being flooded by the tides.

mangrove roots. It has pouches behind its gills that it can fill with water. As long as the gills are wet, they can absorb oxygen from the air.

Because marshes and mangroves are so rich in nutrients, they provide food for a vast number of fish. Flounder, striped bass, and bluefish, as well as many other important food fish, use these wetlands as a nursery, for shelter, and as feeding grounds. Menhaden and mullet, which are eaten by many larger species of fish, regularly feed in the small streams that lace these areas. Scientists estimate that 70 percent of the most important fish of the Atlantic coast use salt marshes at one time or another in their life cycles.

The productivity of salt marshes and mangrove swamps is felt far beyond their borders. The nutrients they produce, and the animals they feed and shelter, contribute to the richness of the waters on the continental shelf.

TIDE POOLS: MINIATURE OCEANS

When the tide goes out along a rocky coast, water is trapped in bowl-like depressions in the rock. These depressions are known as tide pools. Some of them are puddle-size, while others are many feet, even yards, in diameter.

In many ways, tide pools are like miniature oceans. Each one has its own community of animals and, sometimes, plants—although it may vanish when the tide comes in again. Some tide pools are kaleidoscopes of color, splashed with the greens, reds, purples, and oranges of such creatures as sea anemones and sponges. Often, sponges house other creatures. Tucked in its porous tissues, colonies of soft little animals called tunicates may grow. Tiny kelp crabs and anemones the size of pinheads also often live within the channels that honeycomb a sponge's body.

The water of a tide pool, like that of the ocean, contains a network of organisms that are linked by their feeding habits. Such a network is called a food web. In a tide pool, algae and one-celled organisms called diatoms grow by the process of photosynthesis, using the energy of sunlight. Barnacles, periwinkles, and mussels eat the algae and the diatoms. Sea stars feed on mussels, while dog whelk snails consume barnacles and periwinkles. Gulls feed on many tide-pool creatures, including the dog whelks. As happens in the ocean, when tide-pool organisms die, they decay, returning nutrients to the water.

Different colors and varieties of sea stars and anemones fill these tide pools at Point of Arches, in Washington State.

3

Life in Offshore Waters

The rivers that carry nutrients into both the salt marshes and mangrove swamps also help enrich the waters above the continental shelf. Minerals and other particles taken from the land sink to the bottom and become part of the vast storehouse of nutrients on the shelf. These nutrients make the waters of the shelf richer in life than any other area of the earth. Sea creatures large and small gather there to gorge themselves, often on one another. Gray whales devour small crustaceans and fish. Harbor seals chase fish and squid. Vast schools of Atlantic mackerel sweep through the water near the surface, feeding on plankton, small fish, and many other creatures.

Opposite: **Beautiful coral** **reefs are found** **in tropical waters** **and surround** **some tropical** **islands.**

Sea robins use underside chest fins to gather food. They can also unfold large, bright wings to confuse and threaten predators.

On rock piles, tautogs—also called blackfish—crush the shells of mussels and crabs and feed on them. Shellfish are also the prey of skates and rays, which glide close to the bottom in search of food. Sea robins, scuttling along the bottom sand and mud on chest fins shaped like fingers, search for shrimp, crabs, and sea worms. The oyster toadfish, another bottom dweller, feeds on similar prey, and just about any other creature it can get into its gaping mouth. People get much of their food from the continental shelf, too. About 90 percent of the fish caught for human food—cod and haddock, for example—come from the shimmering waters of the shelf.

The Pastures of the Sea

Some scientists have estimated that the ocean above the continental shelf contains the largest number of animals on Earth. The waters are almost thick with living things—plants, animals, and simple organisms, such as one-celled, plantlike diatoms. According to other estimates, green plants in these waters produce more oxygen than all the forests on land do. Most of these plants, which are called phytoplankton, are tiny, and barely—in some cases, not at all—visible to the naked eye. Together with the diatoms, which resemble amoebas in glassy armor, they are the key strand in the food web of the ocean. They make the waters of the continental shelf the lush pastures of the sea.

FAR WANDERERS

Among the great travelers in nature are several species of birds that spend almost all of their lives flying above the sea or resting on its surface. Albatross, shearwaters, and petrels come ashore only to nest. Wandering albatross have a wingspan of 11 feet (3.3 meters), the largest of any bird. Most albatross live in the seas between Antarctica and the Tropic of Capricorn, which are swept continuously by westerly winds. They can glide for days, hardly flapping their wings, by riding on the air currents that rise from the surface of the sea. After the albatross gain altitude they coast for a while, then descend toward the water, bank, and pick up another current. In this way, albatross often fly completely around the world.

Shearwaters and petrels are other seabirds that take advantage of air currents for long-distance travel. Giant petrels live in the same region as albatross and, like them, use the steady westerly winds to circle the globe. Slender-billed shearwaters nest on the islands off southern Australia when it is spring there and autumn in the Northern Hemisphere. By the time young shearwaters are ready to travel, winter is approaching. Both the young and the adults begin an immense journey, actually circling the Pacific Ocean. They head toward Asia, skim by Japan, and then turn toward Alaska. By then, it is summer in the Northern Hemisphere. As they travel, the shearwaters begin to head south, just off of the western coast of North America. By breeding season, they are back in the Australian islands, ready to produce another generation of wide-ranging travelers.

A wandering albatross sweeps across an Antarctic sea.

All of the ocean's organisms are linked by food chains, through which energy is passed from one organism to another. Nutrients from the land, and decomposing plants and animals in the sea, accumulate on the ocean bottom. In turn, these materials promote the growth of phytoplankton, which, like other green plants, capture the energy of sunlight to make food. Microscopic and near-microscopic animals, called zooplankton, eat the phytoplankton, and the energy is passed on to

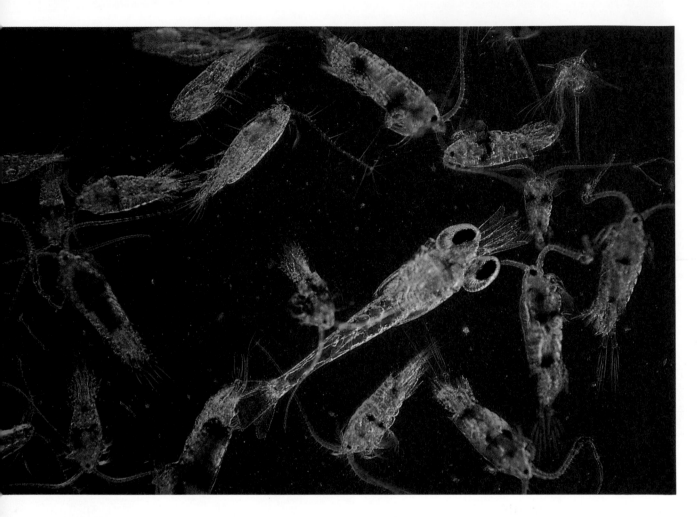

Zooplankton, seen here through the use of a microscope, are an essential part of the ocean food chain.

them. Energy continues to move along the chain as tiny young fish, crustaceans, and other creatures that make up zooplankton are eaten by larger ones. For example, herrings are the food of bluefish, which in turn are eaten by sharks.

Most animals eat a wide variety of foods, and food chains overlap, creating the ocean's food web. Small, shrimplike krill are eaten by many fish—and also by the largest animal on Earth, the great blue whale. Herrings are not only the food of bluefish, but are also eaten directly by sharks and seabirds. Even though organisms die, the food chains, and the food web itself, are not broken. Dead organic matter decomposes into nutrients, and the process continues in a never-ending cycle.

Treasure from the Deep

One reason the waters of the continental shelf have become the sea's pastures is that they are shallow enough for sunlight to penetrate them. Plants need sunlight to provide the energy for photosynthesis, which enables them to grow. Another reason is the process of upwelling, which causes a treasure of nutrients to be churned up from the bottom to the sunlit waters near the surface, where plants abound.

Upwelling can be caused by seasonal temperature changes, storms, winds, and currents. It occurs mostly in cool to cold seas. Warm water is not as dense as cold water, so a warm layer will float on top of a cold one. During the winter, surface waters lose heat. As they become colder than the waters far below they sink, and the deeper waters rise, carrying nutrients up with them. Winter storms also bring nutrients up from the bottom. As the surface waters warm and are bathed in sunlight during spring, diatoms grow and reproduce by the billions. The animals that eat them also thrive, and all continental shelf life increases. The process slows down in summer as the density of the surface waters declines, but as fall moves into winter, it begins again. Upwelling seldom occurs in warm, tropical seas because the surface waters never cool, so few nutrients rise from the bottom.

Cold, Rich Seas

Because cold seas are so rich in nutrients, they produce more phytoplankton and zooplankton than warm waters do. One reason that tropical waters are so clear is the scarcity of plankton. The abundance of plankton in cold waters, however, supports a vast amount of animal life. Tropical seas may contain more species of fish, but because food is so abundant in colder waters, the sheer numbers of fish there are far greater. Many large whales are also more numerous in Arctic and Antarctic waters than elsewhere, because these areas are chock-full of krill and other food eaten by the huge sea mammals.

THE KELP FOREST

Kelp are among the best-known seaweeds. They grow in cold seas and have tough, rubbery stems and wide, ribbonlike fronds. The vine kelp, found in the Pacific Ocean off Chile, anchors on the sea bottom and reaches the surface, more than 250 feet (76 meters) above. Like the rockweeds, kelp float by means of air bladders.

Off the west coast of North America, from Alaska to Mexico, giant kelp, which can reach lengths of 150 feet (46 meters), grow. They form vast, floating "forests" in the sea. Their brown fronds entwine, forming thick mats just offshore that cover hundreds of square miles. On the surface, kelp mats can be so thick that waterbirds can stand on them.

For a scuba diver, moving through a kelp forest is like traveling through a jungle. The heavy fronds are always in the way, and divers must be careful not to become entangled in them. It is a dark world, a little scary to someone seeing it for the first time. However, the trip is worth the fright. The kelp forest is home to many fascinating creatures, such as the reddish-orange Garibaldi fish and the many-hued giant kelpfish. Barnacles stick to the fronds, and spiny lobsters crawl among the holdfasts. During the spring, large schools of fish called opaleyes gather in the kelp off the California and Baja California coasts. Sea urchins also feed heavily on kelp, and sometimes they become so numerous, they can actually destroy the kelp beds.

A forest of giant kelp, off the coast of Southern California.

When the winds and currents are just right, upwelling may occur all year long. A few miles off the coast of Peru, for example, winds from the west interact with the cold Humboldt Current circulating from Antarctica. Vast schools of anchovies feed on phytoplankton within sight of shore. Commercial fishermen catch the anchovies by the millions of tons. Sometimes the wind changes and disrupts currents, blocking upwelling. This happens every few years to the Humboldt Current. When Humboldt Current upwelling was interrupted in 1972, the anchovy population dwindled. Fishermen caught fewer of them and the price of chicken in the United States increased as the price of anchovies, which are used in poultry feed, went up.

A school of anchovies, with gaping mouths, feed on phytoplankton.

37

A huge variety of sea life is sustained in a coral reef. This reef will be even more colorful at night, when the polyps are extended.

Fish Cities

On the continental shelf and around islands in tropical and subtropical seas, 68 million square miles (176 million square kilometers) are covered with coral reefs. Coral is a limy material secreted by polyps—small, soft relatives of jellyfish and sea anemones. The polyps that make these reefs live only in waters with temperatures above 70° F (21° C). Polyps need sunlight, so reefs are scarce below a depth of 150 feet (46 meters), even in crystal-clear tropical waters. Some reefs are small, while others are immense. The largest reef, Australia's Great Barrier Reef, covers over 80,000 square miles (207,200 square kilometers). Reefs grow in size as polyps die and others build more coral over the old.

The polyps take in calcium carbonate from seawater and convert it to coral. A reef can contain billions of living polyps, each one of which makes a cup of coral around it. By day, the coral shelters the polyps. During the night, the polyps extend their tentacles to catch tiny creatures and other bits of food.

Coral reefs are home to many different kinds of creatures. In the cracks and crannies of the reef, octopuses hunt crabs, and moray eels snake into the holes to hunt octopuses. A reef can truly be a fish city. The many shapes and structures of the coral and the small animals living there provide both shelter and food for a host of fish, many of which are brightly colored. Butterfly fish flit in and out of crevices. Their bodies, like dinner plates standing on their edges, allow them to squeeze into small spots in order to escape enemies and to feed. Tiny fish called wrasses graze on minute organisms in the coral. Larger fish hunt the wrasses. One of the most colorful reef fish is the lionfish, of the Indian and Pacific oceans, which is gorgeously striped in maroon and cream. It is slow moving, often hovering in the water. Large fish that would otherwise try

A lionfish extends its sharp spines to fend off a predator.

to eat it generally leave the lionfish alone. If another creature comes near it, the lionfish raises long spines on top of its backbone. The spines are needle-sharp and venomous. If they penetrate another animal—or, for that matter, a person—they can cause extreme pain or even death. The vivid stripes of the lionfish are called warning coloration, a signal to other animals to steer clear. Many creatures that use a chemical defense have warning coloration. How many people, for instance, know to stay away from the skunk, with its black and white warning stripes?

Going to School

In the waters above a coral reef in the Caribbean Sea, a shimmering, silvery form, which from a distance could be a large fish, streaks by. It turns suddenly, then heads in another direction. Close up, the shape turns out to be thousands of tightly packed finger-length fish called reef silversides. They all move as one, which gives the impression of a single large animal. This discourages predators that might be tempted to snack on the small silversides.

The group of silversides together forms a school. Reef silversides are among 4,000 fish that swim in schools, although not all do so throughout their life cycles. A school is a group of fish that swim in unison without a leader. Schooling fish can be found all over the ocean, as well as in fresh water.

Scientists believe that there are several advantages to schooling. Fooling predators is one of them. If members of a school are spread out, the approach of a predator may bring them together so that they appear to be a single animal. This does not always work, however. Some predators, such as bluefish, will careen into a school of prey, cutting the fish to pieces. Schooling enables fish to combine their eyes and other senses to find food. When one member of a school turns toward food, the rest turn with it, and all may benefit from the senses of one.

Wide-Open Spaces

Compared with the continental shelf and its abundant food sources, and with the coral reefs and their countless niches, the wide-open spaces of the ocean beyond the shelf are poor in both plants and animals. Few nutrients from the land reach the open ocean, so plankton is sparse. Plant growth in some parts of the open ocean is only a fraction of that in shelf waters, so food is more difficult to find. With the sea bottom thousands and thousands of feet below, places to hide hardly exist in the sunlit waters near the surface. But some creatures of the open sea, including certain jellyfish and comb jellies, are able to conceal themselves because their bodies are almost as transparent as the water. This does not, however, always protect them from being eaten by the giant ocean sunfish, a slow-moving creature that can weigh up to 4,000 pounds (1,816 kilograms).

SMELLING THE WAY HOME

In the center of the northern Atlantic Ocean, currents that circle between the Americas and Europe and Africa have corralled a vast area of floating seaweed. Called the Sargasso Sea, this area is the breeding ground of the American and European eels, which as adults live in the fresh waters and estuaries of both continents.

As the time to reproduce approaches, adult eels start a journey to the Sargasso, where they were hatched up to fifteen years before. Although the trip can cover as many as 4,000 miles (6,436 kilometers), the eels arrive right on target. Scientists suspect that they smell their way home. Eels have a phenomenal sense of smell. They can detect the odor of a single molecule of certain chemicals in millions of gallons of water. It appears that they somehow pick up the scent of the place in which they began life and simply return there. Currents, too, probably play a part in the eels' navigation. After hatching, the small eels ride the currents until they diverge: American eels set off for North America, and their European relatives head for Europe.

Two truly gargantuan species of shark are frequently seen while feeding near the surface. Whale sharks, which are the largest fish in the world, sometimes reach lengths of 60 feet (18 meters). That is about as long as two basketball courts placed end to end! Despite its size, the whale shark eats tiny crustaceans, as well as small squid and fish. The basking shark, which is 45 feet (14 meters) long, feeds on the even smaller plankton. Both species of shark strain their food from the water with structures called gill rakers, which are located in the area of their gills.

Because they swim at high speeds, such fish as tuna and swordfish are frequently found far offshore. Giant bluefin tuna sometimes swim across the Pacific Ocean from the west coast of North America to Asia. Mako sharks, which are common in parts of the continental shelf, also roam the open ocean, hunting other fish, including tuna and swordfish.

4

The Ocean Depths

Far below the sunlit surface of the open ocean lies the abyss—a place as hostile to humans as deep, dark space. It is a place of eternal blackness, darker than the darkest night, absolutely without light. It is cold, with temperatures in some places below freezing, although ice does not form because salt retards the formation of ice crystals. Water pressure is enormous—up to 8 tons (7 metric tons) per square inch in the deepest areas. That sort of pressure would turn an unprotected human to jelly. The water pressure at a depth of 16,000 feet (4,480 meters) is 530 times greater than that at the surface, and the ocean is twice as deep in some places. Every 33 feet (10 meters) of depth adds 15 pounds (7 kilograms) of pressure per square inch. The human body can tolerate only three times

Opposite:
The black sea
dragon is one of
the gruesome
sea creatures of
the deep. Here,
a dragon dangles
a body part
called a fishing
lure to attract
prey.

the surface pressure, yet even the deepest parts of the abyss are populated by living things (for the most part relatives of animals found in shallower waters). In fact, since 90 percent of the ocean is more than 3,000 feet (915 meters) deep, the abyss is the largest living environment on Earth.

Food from Above

Because there is no light in the deep sea, plants cannot grow, although one-celled algae have been discovered at great depths. Nonetheless, plant matter is still the key to the food web in the deep sea. During the night, many kinds of deep-sea creatures, including tiny crustaceans, squid, and small fish, rise from the depths to feed on plankton near the surface. Like fictional vampires, they retreat to their dark lair with the coming of day. These creatures, in turn, become food for larger ones.

Another source of food in the depths is the remains of dead plants and animals that sink to the bottom; even fragments of land plants that have been washed out to sea end up there. Sinking dead organisms are like a cafeteria for deep-sea creatures, which grab whatever food they can as it drifts by. The small amount of organic matter that finally reaches the sea bed is consumed by bacteria in the mud, which are themselves eaten by such creatures as worms and sea cucumbers. Thus, the food web takes shape as predators eat other animals and are eaten themselves.

The Big Squeeze

There is no mystery about how deep-sea creatures are able to survive the force of tremendous water pressure: Their bodies are made up mostly of water, like other animals, only more so. The bodies of many deep-sea fish, for instance, are almost as watery as those of a jellyfish. It is practically impossible to squeeze water, so the body fluids of deep-sea creatures push back against the squeeze of outside water pressure. Many deep-sea fish also have the ability to travel to within a

ON THE BOTTOM

By and large, creatures that live in the abyss are related to those that inhabit the bottom of shallower waters. Sea fans, for instance, are found on the bottom of the depths, just as they are on coral reefs. Bristleworms that live in the mud of the abyss are related to earthworms. Sea stars, or starfish, inhabit the bottom, as do hermit crabs. Some hermit crabs carry sea anemones on their bodies. The stinging tentacles of the anemones provide a defense for the crabs, which take some of the food caught by the anemones.

Some fish spend all their lives on the deep-sea floor. Generally, they are rather poor swimmers. Rattails, cousins of the codfish, are very common on the sea bottom. Rattails get their name from their long, thin tails. A rattail's snout is pointed, and its head is covered with sense organs that can pick up the movement of other animals in the water. The tubelike mouth of a rattail is under its head, and its chin has feelers that resemble a beard. Scientists believe that rattails dig in the mud with their snouts, using their feelers and sense organs to locate crustaceans, sponges, and other small animals for food.

Perhaps the most intriguing animals of the deep ocean floor are beard worms, which are not really worms at all, just wormlike in form. Their scientific name is Pogonophora. These creatures, discovered in 1900, constitute an entire phylum of the animal kingdom. In comparison, the million species of anthropods—which includes insects, crustaceans, and spiders—make up a single phylum. No one knows for sure how many species of Pogonophora exist, but it is certainly only a handful. These wormlike creatures live in tubes in the mud, extending tentacles to feed. Lacking a mouth and a digestive system, beard worms absorb and digest food in their tentacles.

few hundred feet of the surface. As a fish rises, and water pressure decreases, the gases in its swim bladder expand. The swim bladder swells and is in danger of exploding. By rising slowly, and absorbing gases from the bladder into its blood, a fish traveling upward from the depths can prevent itself from becoming too large. Nor is cold a problem for the animals of the abyss: Their normal body temperatures are similar to that of the water around them.

Monsters and Mini-Monsters

A few animals that live in the ocean depths are huge, such as the monstrous giant squids that are almost 60 feet (18 meters) long. The Greenland shark, about 20 feet (6 meters) long, sometimes inhabits waters almost 4,000 feet (1,220 meters) deep. However, in the true depths, almost all of the creatures are small, even tiny. Many jellyfish that live there are less than an inch across. There is a blind, deep-sea octopus that is only about as long as an adult's finger. Many anglerfish of the abyss are only a couple of inches long. Some lantern fish are less than 2 inches (5 centimeters) long and weigh only a gram.

Small as they may be, however, many of these fish look—and act—like mini-monsters. The saber-toothed viper-fish, which ranges from 2 to 12 inches (5 to 30 centimeters) long, resembles the mother alien in the film *Alien*. Its gaping jaws are lined with fangs so long that scientists are unsure

A grisly viperfish chases a hatchet-fish, which has light organs around the edges of its body.

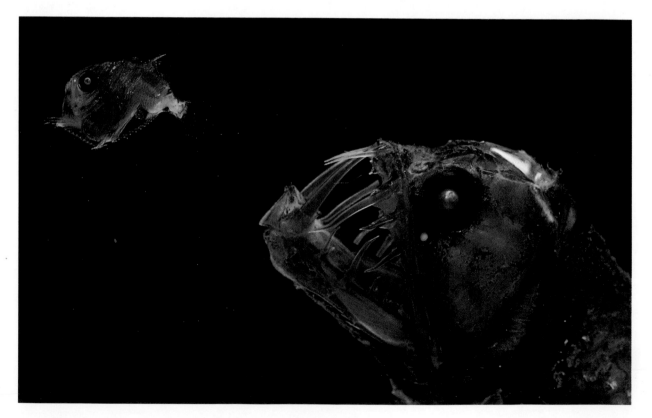

whether the fish can completely close its mouth. The jaws are attached to powerful muscles that give the fish a fearsome bite. Like the viperfish, the black swallower and the gulper also have jaws that extend far to the back of their heads and open like yawning pits. There is a reason for those jaws. These three fishes are fierce predators, designed for quickly eating food that is hard to get at in the deep. The black swallower, only a few inches long, can engulf prey as much as three times its length. Not surprisingly, the swallower's stomach can expand.

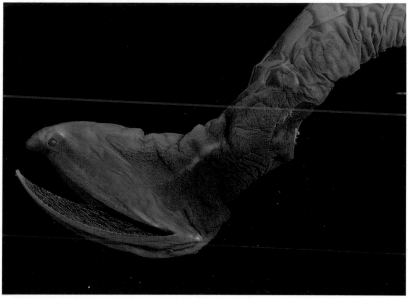

The profile of a swallower shows its deep jaws, which reach practically to the back of its head.

Most of the fishes that qualify as mini-monsters are good swimmers, even if they do move rather slowly. They generally live in waters between 6,000 feet (1,830 meters) and 12,000 feet (3,660 meters) deep, although some are also found at greater ocean depths.

Deep-Sea Fireworks

Anyone who has seen a firefly flashing in the summer night knows that some animals can produce light, or bioluminescence. Many—perhaps most—deep-sea animals have that ability, and they produce some real fireworks in the pitch-black abyss. Bioluminescence results from a chemical reaction in which a substance called luciferin combines with oxygen to generate energy in the form of light. The reaction is controlled by another substance, luciferase. Many deep-sea creatures produce the reaction on their own, in special cells. Others carry colonies of light-producing bacteria on their bodies and can turn them on with a flow of oxygen-bearing blood. Either way, the light is created in organs called photophores, which are usually cup-shaped.

Photophores are located on many different parts of the bodies of deep-sea animals, but they appear mostly on the sides and bellies. Long-bodied fish called stomatoids bear rows of circular light spots that run down their sides. Some squid have light spots at the tips of their tentacles. Shrimplike krill have red spots on their sides and at the top of their eyestalks. Bioluminescent deep-water animals can put on a real show.

CLASH OF THE TITANS (DUEL IN THE DEPTHS)

The sperm whale is the most awesome creature in the ocean. With a massive head and powerful jaws lined with teeth up to 6 inches (15 centimeters) long, the 60-foot (18-meter) long sperm whale hunts the giant squid. The largest of living invertebrates (animals without backbones), the giant squid can be almost as long as the sperm whale, although most of its length is accounted for by two long tentacles, whose paddlelike tips are studded with powerful suckers. The squid's arms, which can be almost as thick as a telephone pole and 12 feet (4 meters) long, also bear suckers—thousands of them. Both the tentacles and the arms are used to grab prey and draw it into the squid's sharp, hooked beak.

Sperm whales eat many animals, including sharks, but their main food is squid, mostly small ones. Sometimes, however, these mighty whales stalk the giant squid, a creature whose habits are as mysterious as the dark depths it inhabits. Seldom rising above 600 feet (183 meters), giant squid descend far deeper—in fact, thousands of feet deeper.

Scientists know that sperm whales can dive to depths of 3,000 feet (915 meters) and stay below for almost an hour. They also have evidence that these whales wage titanic battles against giant squid in the undersea blackness. The evidence? The hides of sperm whales often bear the marks of wounds inflicted by monstrous suckers, those of the giant squid. The question is, who attacks whom? While a giant squid might not turn down a small whale for dinner, it appears that the sperm whale is the one that goes after the squid. The remains of giant squids have turned up in the stomachs of sperm whales, but sperm whales have never been found in the stomachs of giant squids.

Most of the light they emit is bluish green, but it can also include purple, red, yellow, and white. Some animals are always lit up; others blink, flash, or set off star bursts.

Living light has many uses. Some krill have large round lights, like a car's headlamps, above their eyes. The lights rotate when the eyes do and probably help the krill to see food and enemies. Anglerfish use lighted, fleshy tabs and rods (often called fishing lures) as bait to attract prey. On land, males and females of different species of fireflies identify one another by signal flashes. Scientists believe that many deep-sea creatures also use light as a mating signal. Light is probably also used as a defense against predators. When attacked, certain deep-sea shrimp release a dazzling cloud of light specks, which may confuse its enemies and allow them to escape.

A deep-sea anglerfish attracts two shrimp with its lighted lure.

5

Threats to the Sea

As vast as it is, the ocean environment, like that of the land biomes of Earth, is being damaged by human activities. No one can deny that people need food to eat, places to live, and fuel to burn. And that every second, there are more and more people on Earth who need these things. But there are issues that we should be able to deal with safely, without harming the very environment that supports us. Life originally began in the ocean. If human beings continue to destroy ocean life, then all life on Earth will be in danger.

Opposite: This herring gull, entangled in a plastic six-pack yoke, is a victim of ocean pollution.

Threats from the Land

Just as the land contributes minerals and other nutrients to the sea, it is also the source of pollutants that harm the ocean environment. So closely are all of the earth's biomes bound together, that changes caused by people well inland can sometimes be felt far out to sea. One source of pollution is called runoff, and it can happen in urban as well as farming areas. During heavy rains, road salt, oils, industrial wastes, overflowing sewage, and solid waste can be swept into city storm sewers. If the sewers drain into streams, they may ultimately empty into the ocean.

Pesticides running off farmland are just as bad, perhaps even worse. More than sixty agricultural pesticides have been found in the drinking water of people in fourteen states, including coastal states in the middle Atlantic and the southeast regions. These pesticides threaten human health—they are thought to increase the risk of cancer. Pesticides can also end up in the ocean. The Chesapeake Bay area of Maryland and

Wastewater from a coal strip mine runs into waters near the coast of Virginia.

Virginia is one of the places where pesticides have turned up in drinking water. Nitrogen from fertilizers and farm-animal waste has also polluted the ocean. Nitrogen stimulates the growth of algae to levels at which these organisms use up all the oxygen in the water. Without oxygen, fish die. Moreover, dangerous gasses build up, killing even more fish. Industrial waste, including toxic chemicals, has long been discharged into the sea. However, an increasing number of new laws and regulations—in addition to environmentally responsible actions taken by many industries—are reducing this threat to the ocean biome.

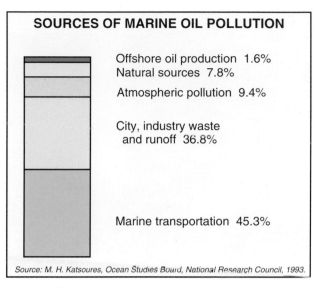

SOURCES OF MARINE OIL POLLUTION

Offshore oil production 1.6%
Natural sources 7.8%

Atmospheric pollution 9.4%

City, industry waste and runoff 36.8%

Marine transportation 45.3%

Source: M. H. Katsoures, Ocean Studies Board, National Research Council, 1993.

Chemical pollutants cause a Pandora's box of problems. They make the environment generally unhealthy. They poison and cause disease in fish and other marine creatures. A pollutant has only to destroy one organism in order to threaten others throughout the sea's food web.

Siltation is another major problem. As rivers carry soil from land to water, silt builds up on the bottom. Some silt reaches inshore waters. This is a natural process, but poor land management has made siltation a danger to aquatic life. Scientists believe that the natural rate of siltation in the sea is about 10 billion tons (9 billion metric tons) a year. Now, silt accumulates at about 25 billion tons (23 billion metric tons) annually.

Poor conservation policies in the lumber industry of the Pacific Northwest are not only destroying some of the last great forests, but are creating siltation that threatens the Pacific salmon. Adult salmon, which live at sea, migrate upriver to mate and lay their eggs. Many of these streams lie in the middle of areas that are being logged for timber. In many

places, timber companies use a technique called clear-cutting. Every single tree in an area is cut down, leaving a wasteland that looks as if a bomb had exploded there. Without trees to break the forces of wind and rain, soil washes away from the clear-cut areas into salmon streams. The silt from eroded soil clogs the water, as well as the gills of the salmon. Worse, it smothers the salmon's eggs. Because of both siltation and hydroelectric dams, several species of Pacific salmon are disappearing.

Dangers at Sea

Almost three quarters of the petroleum produced by oil wells is shipped on ocean-going tankers. Oil tankers all too frequently have accidents, and petroleum floods the sea. Oil coats seabirds, so they cannot fly. It also enters the digestive systems of fish and poisons them, as well as their

This barren hillside is the result of one clear-cut logging operation in Washington State.

eggs. It blankets shellfish, so they cannot breathe. After the *Exxon Valdez* oil spill in 1989, a vast amount of sea life was poisoned. Chemicals in the oil spread throughout the sea. They have even been found in the mud of the abyss. Tanker accidents can release huge amounts of oil into the sea in a matter of hours or days. However, even more oil enters the water from runoff, industrial waste, and other sources on land.

Another source of ocean pollution is the garbage and other waste dumped from ships at sea. Scientists estimate that each year, millions of tons of trash from ships worldwide ends up in the ocean. Plastic bags are a particular problem because they can resemble jellyfish, which are the prey of sea creatures such as the leatherback turtle and the giant ocean sunfish. If they mistake a plastic bag for a jellyfish and eat it, they are likely to die.

These barges will be towed out to sea and the garbage dumped into the water.

SAVING SEA TURTLES

These baby sea turtles have just hatched. You can see fragments of their shells in the sand all around them.

In the dark of a summer night, as starlight glimmers on the surf, a huge head rises from the waves off a Florida beach. Behind the head, a massive shell, enclosing a 300-pound (163-kilogram) body, becomes visible. Slowly the creature, a female loggerhead sea turtle, crawls from the water onto the beach. The turtle has come ashore to lay her eggs in the sand.

Sea turtles lay their eggs on the same beaches on which they were hatched. Many of these beaches, however, have been disturbed by human activities, such as the construction of homes, resorts, and even sea walls. Sea turtles are very cautious creatures. Even a person just walking down the beach may disturb a female turtle as she comes ashore, and send her back into the sea. Once she begins to dig a hole in the sand and lay her eggs there, however, she ignores the presence of people.

The destruction of nesting beaches is just one of the conditions that have threatened sea turtles. Some of them have been overhunted for their beautiful shells and for their flesh. The eggs of sea turtles are eaten in many parts of the world. Sea turtles breathe air, and thousands of them each year get caught in fishing gear and drown.

To help save the sea turtles, an increasing number of nesting beaches are being protected, at least during the time of year the turtles come ashore. Worldwide, there are at least seventy conservation laws covering sea turtles, including the United States Endangered Species Act. Many international agreements also protect sea turtles, although not completely. More and more nations, however, are realizing that if human actions can threaten sea turtles, human actions can also save them.

Overfishing

Saving the great whales from commercial whalers has been a popular cause for many conservationists. Today, most countries observe international agreements that have ended the hunting of most whales, which are making something of a comeback. It is easy for people to like whales because, like humans, they are mammals. But what about fish, including those that people eat? There are no longer plenty of fish in the sea. Many of the world's most important food fish have been caught in such great numbers that they have disappeared. Fishing fleets are high-tech now, using radar, orbiting satellites, and sonar to make their catches. Electronic fish finders can spot a single fish 600 feet (183 meters) deep in the water. Nets are immense; some are large enough to encircle a football field. As a result, the number of adult, bluefin tuna in the Atlantic has fallen by 90 percent since the 1970s. Breeding-age Atlantic swordfish have declined by half. Halibut and haddock seldom turn up in commercial catches anymore. Important fisheries, on which fishermen depend for their livelihoods and people for food, have been depleted.

A positive step to solving the overfishing problem is the success of hatcheries, or fish farms, like this one in Newfoundland, Canada.

FISH FOR THE FUTURE

Fish, mostly from the ocean, are a major source of food for people around the world. Two thirds of the world's human population, almost all of them in poor, developing nations, get 40 percent of their protein from fish. Worldwide, that is about 100 tons (90 metric tons) of fish each year, the protein equivalent of meat from 200 million cattle.

By 1990, fishermen around the globe were catching five times the number of fish that they were catching in the 1950s, even though many of the most important food fish were declining. With this decline, fishermen started focusing on other species and new fishing grounds. Almost all of the decrease has been in the waters of rich, developed countries, such as those off the coasts of New England and southeastern Canada. Faced with a dwindling catch in these waters, fishing fleets from developed countries are increasing their activity in the waters of the Third World. Thus, poor nations that need fish the most stand to lose their fishery resources.

Conservationists propose several ways to reduce overfishing and to allow the number of food fish to increase. Some of these ideas are already being tried. One approach is to limit not only the number of fish a vessel may catch, but the number of boats permitted in a given area. Another is for countries to charge fees for foreigners who fish in their waters. An even more drastic step is to prohibit the harvesting of threatened species until they recover. In the long run, this approach would mean more fish for the future. Scientists estimate that if food-fish populations in the United States' waters returned to their former numbers, fishermen would eventually double their current catch.

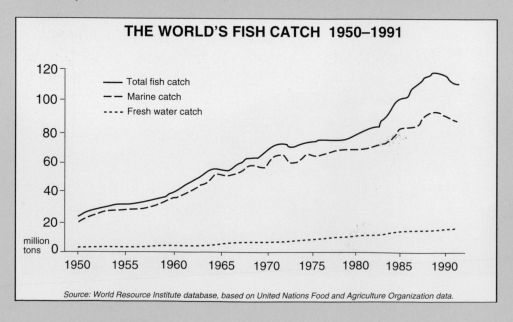

Source: World Resource Institute database, based on United Nations Food and Agriculture Organization data.

Overfishing happens in huge regions of the oceans. It can also occur in a small area. In 1988, scientists discovered a reef off the country of Honduras where 10,000 Nassau groupers gathered to breed. They kept the location secret, but two years later, local fishermen found it. Within a year, only 500 groupers remained, and the coral was battered and littered with trash. Because they were greedy, the fishermen not only wiped out adult groupers that would have produced future generations, they destroyed the habitat the fish needed to breed.

Saving the Sea

Despite the damage to the ocean, the future is not gloomy. Conservation organizations, governments, and other people have recognized the threats to the ocean and are working to correct them. Laws and agreements are being created at local, national, and international levels to protect the ocean environment and to conserve its resources. Many commercial fishermen, for example, now understand that by overfishing, they are eliminating the resource that provides their income. Quotas are being established that limit the number of fish that can be caught, leaving some for the future. The U.S. government continues to toughen regulations covering clean water and waste disposal. As with many other environmental and conservation problems, however, the human population explosion lies at the root of many threats to the ocean. Humans are overcrowding their world and upsetting its natural balances. Unless humanity can address this issue, other environmental problems will continue, and probably worsen.

Glossary

abyss The deepest part of the ocean.

bioluminescence Light that is organically produced by animals.

blowhole The hole, or paired holes, atop the head of a whale, porpoise, or dolphin, through which it breathes.

clear-cutting Indiscriminate cutting of trees that completely levels an area of forest.

continental shelf The submerged lip of land that extends from the edges of the continents into the ocean.

continental slope The region seaward of the continental shelf that slopes to the floor of the abyss.

ecotone A place where two different habitats meet.

fluke The tail of whales, porpoises, and dolphins that is used for swimming power.

food chain The way in which energy is transferred from one organism to another through consumption of food.

food web Interlocking and overlapping food chains.

gill rakers Structures in the gill areas of many fish that allow them to strain food from the water.

gills Structures with which fish and many other aquatic animals obtain oxygen from the water.

holdfast The structure by which kelp and other seaweeds anchor themselves.

intertidal zone The area that is covered and uncovered by the tides.

oceanic ridge A chain of mountains on the ocean floor.

photophore Organs that produce bioluminescence.

phytoplankton Microscopic and near-microscopic aquatic plants.

seamount A mountain that rises from the ocean floor.

swim bladder A gas-filled organ in many fishes that can be inflated and deflated, helping the fish to rise, sink, or stay in place.

upwelling A process through which nutrients are churned up from the ocean bottom.

warning coloration Striking patterns or colors on a creature that warn predators to stay away from it, often on animals that have a chemical defense.

zooplankton Microscopic and near-microscopic aquatic animals.

For Further Reading

Bright, Michael. *The Dying Sea.* New York: Franklin Watts, 1992.

Hopkins, Lee B. *The Sea Is Calling Me.* Florida: Harcourt Brace, 1986.

Lambert, David and McConnell, Anita. *Seas and Oceans.* New York: Facts On File, 1985.

Myerson, A. Lee. *Seawater: A Delicate Balance.* New Jersey: Enslow, 1988.

Robinson, W. Wright. *Incredible Facts About the Ocean, Vol. 3: How We Use It, How We Abuse It.* New York: Dillon, 1990.

Tesar, Jenny. *Threatened Oceans.* New York: Facts On File, 1992.

_____. *What on Earth is a Nudibranch?* Woodbridge, CT: Blackbirch Press, 1995.

_____. *What on Earth is a Sea Squirt?* Woodbridge, CT: Blackbirch Press, 1994.

Williams, Brian. *The Sea.* New York: Franklin Watts, 1991.

Williams, Lawrence. *Oceans.* New York: Marshall Cavendish, 1990.

Index

Acknowledgments and Photo Credits

Cover: ©Chris Huxley/Leo de Wys, Inc.; p. 6: ©Japack/Leo de Wys, Inc.; p. 12 (left): ©Charles V. Angelo/Photo Researchers, Inc.; pp. 12 (right), 13, 32, 37, 42, 46, 47, 49: ©Norbert Wu/Peter Arnold, Inc.; p. 16: ©Gerald Lacz/Animals Animals; p. 18: ©Michael P. Gadomski/Earth Scenes; p. 20: ©Stephen J. Krasemann/Peter Arnold, Inc.; p. 22: ©Nancy Sefton/Photo Researchers, Inc.; p. 24: ©Pat Lynch/Photo Researchers, Inc.; p. 25: ©Stephen J. Krasemann/Photo Researchers, Inc.; p. 28: ©Doug Wechsler/Animals Animals; p. 29: ©Patti Murray/Earth Scenes; p. 30: ©Mickey Gibson/Animals Animals; p. 33: ©Johnny Johnson/Animals Animals; p. 34: ©Manfred Kage/Peter Arnold, Inc.; p. 36: ©Gregory Ochocki/Photo Researchers, Inc.; p. 38: ©W. Gregory Brown/Animals Animals; p. 39: ©Animals Animals; p. 50: ©Fred Bavendam/Peter Arnold, Inc.; p. 52: Kenneth Murray/Photo Researchers, Inc.; p. 54: ©David C. Fritts/Earth Scenes; p. 55: ©Herb Segars/Earth Scenes; p. 56: ©Fred Whitehead/Animals Animals; p. 57: ©Francis Lepine/Earth Scenes.
Artwork and graphics by Blackbirch Graphics, Inc.